Crystals and Gemstones:
Windows of the Self
by Miriam Kaplan

**Cassandra Press
Boulder, CO   80306**

Printed in the United States of America.

First printing 1987

ISBN 0-9615875-3-9

Library of Congress Catalogue Card Number.

87-071832

Front cover photo by Michael Tivana.
Copyright © 1987 Cassandra Press.

TABLE OF CONTENTS

Prologue: The Language of the Stones

Diamond, Corundum Family, Ruby, Sapphire, Blue Sapphire, Yellow Sapphire, Topaz, Tourmaline, Lapis Lazuli, Garnet, Peridot, Amber, Coral, Pearl, Opal, Chalcedony (Agate, Bloodstone, Jasper, Chrysoprase), Green Aventurine, Carnelian, Sard, The Beryl Family (Emerald, Aquamarine, Golden Beryl, Morganite, Goshenite), The Copper Stones, Turquoise, Azurite, Azurite- Malachite, Chrysocolla, Rhodochrosite, Jade, Chrysoberyl

CHAPTER IV:

Prologue

The Language of Stones

If you are truly open to seeing and listening to nature, teachings exist there, and knowledge is revealed. When you work with crystals and other gems, you learn that there is a beautiful language in the stones. As you allow yourself the space just to "be," the stones will speak to you, mirroring your own inner planes of awareness, as well as the outer spheres and dimensions of Light. The language of stones will teach you that there is nothing to hold on to, for everything is in flux. You can only perceive the lessons that they reflect as you live and walk along your path each day.

Chapter I

Crystals and Gemstones: Windows of the Self

Crystals and gemstones have been used since ancient times to heal, to help expand awareness, to protect, to generate energy, for prophecy, and for beauty. We are on the verge of a great shift in consciousness on the planet, and once again crystals and gemstones are coming forth as our helpers. There are many levels and many ways that crystals and gemstones work: Some of these are known now, some will be discovered in the future. This book is a combination of intuitive work I have done with crystals and with gemstones, as well as factual information. The purpose of this book is for you to acquaint yourself with crystals and with gemstones.

As you read the book, please keep in mind that it is written with the intention of helping you attune to these focal points of earth's energy. Because most information about the use of crystals and gemstones lies within our remembrances of very ancient times, the real knowledge of this subject is within you. The only way to know crystals is to listen to them, to learn your own heart, of the teachings that stir from the silence and complete beauty that is inside of you.

The rhythm of the book will include information about crystals and the formation of matter, how the human body responds to crystals and gems, and the history of the use of crystals and gemstones. Information on the correspondence of gemstones and other forms such as astrology will be included. I will talk about the extensive use of crystals, about specific properties of gemstones, of the electromagnetic power spots on the earth, of going to places on the earth to recharge and heal yourself, and of the use of crystals to remind ourselves of where we have been, of our true heritage, and of where we are going. It is my wish that this book serve as a tuning device for your use to augment your own intuitive abilities, your own inner knowing.

As I wrote this book, one main theme became apparent to me in it. That is, that all life is sacred, that all created matter is created in accord with the laws of Light, and that seeded within all matter is the expression of the creator. I feel crystals and gemstones are used as a vehicle because they are focal energy points of the earth, and yet they are aligned to the heavens. They are the bridge between matter and spirit. They exist to remind us of our own brilliance, our own radiance, our own inner light, and our own inner knowing.

The Spiritual Aspect of Creation

Crystals and gemstones are formed by the earth through millions of years of geological activity, through the combination of heat and pressure. Elements from other stars, from other galaxies, are made up in the crystals and gemstones that occurred during the earth's formation. The process of creation always occurs from the spiritual to the physical. This process is overseen by members of the spiritual hierarchy, a hierarchy of beings of Light whose service it is to assist in manifestation. The spiritual hierarchy which performs this creative function works in a triadic unit. This work can be best described as an interfacing of energy, from the most subtle and closest to the inner sun, to the manifestation of matter.

This interfacing of Light is a continuous process, and, in fact, forms the earth's holding pattern so that she can bring forth life in all of its forms. The expression of the earth's creation is holy, her enduring manifestation is holy, and the relationship of humans on this planet is holy. The fulfillment of all created life is to express its sanctity in the way befitting to itself. As we, as a collective group, learn to look within, to still the mind, to pray for assistance from the Divine Love, we attune to understanding the sacredness of the earth and of our way on this earth. As we as a group work together, we learn to walk on this earth in a sacred way. This is completion of the cycle of manifestation, whereby knowledge is made manifest, and the circle becomes complete.

When the cycle is complete, a being—like Jesus who became Christ—can appear in the physical form after his bodily death, as Jesus appeared to Mary. This is a teaching that pure Love can manifest at will in physical form. This is possible only after the form becomes sanctified. In our process of sanctifying our form, our experience on the planet earth, we exist in the body, in embodiment. It is through existing in the body that we come to understand ourselves. It is also because we exist in the body, in embodiment, that we are in correspondence to the mineral, plant, and animal kingdoms, as well as to the solar systems and the galaxies of outer space.

The Law of Correspondence

The Law of Correspondence is a higher law that operates in many dimensions in the universe. The best way of stating this law is to emphasize the interrelatedness among all forms of matter as well as among the higher spheres that assist in bringing matter into manifestation. The ancients understood this law and built their structures, such as Stonehenge or the Pyramids, to correspond with the activity of the Sun, the moon, and the planets. Planting times were established in correspondence with interplanetary events. Rituals were established within the spheres of cosmic events. Ley lines, the type of lines found in the in certain power spots about the Earth were established with correspondence to interplanetary systems. In the plant kingdom, another example of the Law of Correspondence is called the Law of Signatures. That means that the shape, color, and smell of a plant will indicate what organ in the body it will heal.

A basic building energy system underlies all forms of manifestation. Crystals and most gemstones are formed by a crystalline structure that functions as a building block, or building system, in creation. All aspects of creation correspond to each other. When you work with basic building block structures, such as the crystalline structures of stones, you are working in correspondence to a basic form of manifestation from the spiritual to the physical in the universe. Trace elements found within crystals and gemstones are also found within our bodies. When you wear a stone, the trace elements in the stone will work in correspondence to and will stimulate the same trace elements in your body.

Mineralogy and the Origins of Crystals
(Reprinted with permission of Pat Dongvillo)

From the prized flints of the Stone Age, whose magic created fire, to the uranium ores of the Atomic Age and the silicates of today's Communication Age, minerals have contributed vitally to the growth of civilization. We have long recognized the importance of precious metals and stones. Tomb paintings in the Nile Valley nearly 5,000 years old show craftsmen weighing fine metals, smelting mineral ores, and carving emeralds into gems. Minerals are naturally occurring chemical substances that make up rock and stone. They are inorganic substances— they have not been formed by a living process as wood from a tree has. Minerals themselves are composed of one or more of the ninety-odd natural elements in the Earth's crust. The atoms of these elements fit together in certain ways to produce geometrical shapes called crystals. It is these particular crystal structures that make it possible for us to differentiate one mineral from another. Some minerals occur in a pure form, such as Gold, and are known as native substances, but most minerals are chemical compounds.

Some minerals have the same chemical composition (consist of the same elements) but are clearly different minerals because their crystallization process varied considerably. Diamond and Graphite are both forms of carbon but the atoms making up their crystalline structure are arranged entirely differently due to the amount of pressure and temperature on them when they were underground. This difference in crystalline structure of the same element makes Diamond the hardest known mineral, highly used in industry for cutting or abrasive purposes; whereas Graphite is one of the softest, used as the "lead" in pencils and as a lubricant in industry.

Crystals are formed in various ways. Just as ice crystals form when water freezes, crystallization of minerals occurs when molten lava cools. Crystals are even formed from vapors, as in sulfur crystals from the cooling of sulfur-bearing gases around active volcanos. Crystallization can occur from solutions that become so highly saturated that the compound precipitates out as a solid. The great Salt Lake and nearby Salt Flats are good illustrations of a crystallization from a solution of sodium chloride dissolved in water. As the water is evaporated, the solution contains more and more salt per volume of water. Eventually, the time comes when the remaining water can no longer hold all the salt in solution, and solid salt begins to precipitate. If the process of evaporation is very slow, or the cooling is slow as in the case of molten lava, larger crystals with more characteristic shapes will be formed.

Today, many types of crystals are produced synthetically for use in electronics and other industries. Synthetics are the only feasible alternative when large quantities of crystals with consistent qualities are needed or when the mineral is rare, such as Diamonds. Synthetic crystals are produced in much the same way as nature produces crystals, except that everything is controlled to meet certain specifications: the composition is predetermined, ovens or heating elements are used, and methods for cooling the substance at certain rates are employed. Artificial Ruby is made by melting a powder of specified composition in a flame and letting it fall to a surface where the crystal will grow as it cools.

Most crystallographers use the term crystal in reference to any solid with an ordered internal structure, regardless of whether it possesses external faces. This usage is within reason, as the destruction of what appear to be the boundary faces in no way changes the fundamental properties of the crystal. It is however the morphology, the external geometry, that most enthusiasts are attracted to initially. In this sense, the crystal is viewed in the mind's eye as a regular geometric solid bounded by smooth plane surfaces.

There are many, many wonderful crystals in

the mineral kingdom. The different properties of crystals are as varied as the combinations of elements they are made of. There are so many combinations that broad divisions of classification have been created such as the native elements mentioned earlier, where we find singularly occurring elements such as the metals of Gold, Silver, Copper, Iron and nonmetals such as Sulfur, Diamond, and Graphite. Other classifications have been created because of the dominance of particular elements in the minerals: carbon in the carbonates, nitrogen in the nitrates, phosphates, oxides, etc. In the oxide minerals we find those natural compounds in which oxygen is combined with one or more metals. Corundum is often the subject of a popular novel or motion picture. We may not readily recognize it as an oxide of aluminum, but depending on the crystal's color it may be a ruby. If it is blue and has a certain stellate opalescence when viewed in the direction of one of the crystal's axes, it may even be a star sapphire.

The crystals found in the silicate mineral class are of the greatest interest today in the "crystal movement." The most common, and often the most popular, is that known as Quartz crystal. Quartz Crystal in its pure form is totally clear, in contrast to other members of the Quartz family such as Rose Quartz, Milky Quartz, Smoky Quartz, Amethyst, and others. Quartz belongs to the family of minerals called silicates. Silicates are minerals that contain silica and oxygen in combination with other minerals or in a pure state as free silica. Pure quartz, SiO_2, is free silica. Of every 100 atoms in the crust of the earth, more than 60 are oxygen, over 20 silicon, and six or seven are aluminum. Iron, calcium, magnesium, sodium, and potassium each account for approximately two more atoms. The silicates make up 25% of the known minerals and nearly 40% of the common ones. With a few exceptions all the igneous rock-forming (rocks formed from the cooling and hardening of hot molten rock) minerals are silicates, thereby constituting well over 90% of the earth's crust.

The soil from which our food is ultimately drawn is made up in large part of silicates; the brick, stone, concrete, and glass used in the construction of our buildings, as well as the beaches we stroll, on are comprised of silicates. A 150 pound man contains about 1-1/4 ounce of silicon. Silicon is found in all animal and vegetable tissues. It gives firmness to stalks of grains and produces a polished, hard outside surface on oats, barley, rice, corn, and other cereals. It also gives the hardness, firmness, elasticity, and polish to the bones, teeth, and tendons of animals and human beings. Just as silicon supports the outer linings of many foods in the plant kingdom, it similarly protects the outside linings of animals and humans. Nails, hair, and skin derive their sheen, resilience, and smoothness from silicon. If silicon is found lacking in any of these, it will be deficient throughout the body.

Silicon is known as the "magnetic element" because of its powerful electrical charge that always is ready to combine it with other elements. In all living beings, nerve transmission would be impossible without silicon. As part of the nervous system, silicon carries the electrical nerve impulses, or messages of the brain, to the various destinations in the body. So it is quite natural that in industry today we find silicon in its crystalline form of pure quartz (that which makes up Quartz Crystal) being used in all facets of image and message transmission.

Because of its transparency in both the infrared and ultraviolet portions of the spectrum and its ability to rotate the plane of polarization of light, quartz is made into lenses and prisms for optical instruments. It is because of its piezoelectric properties (the ability of Quartz Crystals to receive and transmit frequencies) that it has attracted so much attention. In our modern day, the ability of Quartz Crystals to communicate precise frequencies has made satellite, telephone, radio, and television communications possible. We find science using this crystal oscillation phenomenon, or technology developed from it, in all manner of electronic devices, from computers to quartz time pieces.

Because of the common link of silicon in all living plants and beings and the beingness of our planet, we find today a re-emergence of a more personal attraction between the crystal and man. Quartz Crystal has been held in special esteem over the ages. In many cultures, both east and west, the crystal was considered a powerful sacred object capable of divination and healing.

The Crystalline Structure of Crystals and Gemstones

The crystalline structure of crystals and gemstones is in fact a crystallized form of the energy of Light which is the same energy that manifests all creation. All gemstones—except Amber, Jet, Coral, Pearl, and Opal—are actually "crystals" because they are formed from a crystalline structure. There are six crystalline systems that distinguish gemstones: the Cubic, Hexagonal, Tetragonal, Orthorhombic, Triclinic, and Monoclinic. There has existed since very ancient times a sacred science that reveals the meaning and correspondences of numbers, of forms, and of measurements. Perhaps if you take the time to meditate on each crystalline system, the secrets of its structure in correspondence to the human body, the energy systems, and the vibration of the stones will be revealed to you.

CUBIC

The cubic system is the most simple crystal-line structure of the six. Diamond, Garnet, Lapis Lazuli, and Fluorite are all formed within this system.

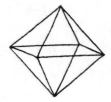

HEXAGONAL

Quartz Crystals come from this second most simple crystalline structure. Ruby and Sapphire (the Corundum family), Tourmaline, Rhodochro-site, Beryl (Emerald, Aquamarine, Golden Beryl, and Morganite), and Chalcedony (Agate, Blood-stone, Jasper, and Carnelian, etc.) are all formed within the hexagonal system.

TETRAGONAL

The Zircon and Idocrase are formed in this third system:

ORTHORHOMBIC

This crystalline structure includes the Chrysoberyl (the Cat's Eye and Alexandrite), Peridot, Topaz, and Iolite:

TRICLINIC

The Rhodonite and the Feldspar family (the

Labradorite and Moonstone) are found in this system:

MONOCLINIC

The sixth crystalline structure includes the Diopside, Jadeite, Malachite, and Nephrite:

The Rainbow Way:
Colors In Gemstones

"We are the rainbow people
We walk the path with heart
This is the blessing way. Ho."

Aside from Clear Quartz, Diamond, White Topaz, and Goshenite (a colorless Beryl), most gemstones radiate color. Stones like Quartz Crystals, and such colorless stones as the Topaz, often exhibit rainbows. It has long been known that the American Indians meditated with the healing colors of the rainbow that emanate from crystals to help their dying transcend the physical realm. Many who have studied the healing power of gems and color therapy have experienced that each of these rainbow colors emits a distinct vibratory ray that is beneficial to the body and the psyche.

There are seven color rays: red, pink, orange, yellow, green, blue, and purple. Before turning to other aspects of gemstones, it is valuable to pay at least brief homage to these dynamic rays by presenting some of the characteristics inherent in each color vibration:

RED

Red activates the energies of the body and stimulates the circulatory system and the heart. It gives vitality, courage, and strength.

PINK

The color of universal Love, pink benefits the heart and removes sorrows and past hurts.

This color attunes you to love's soothing presence in all of creation.

ORANGE

The stimulating color, orange, strengthens the nervous system. It also aids digestion and the glandular system of the body. A special feature of orange is its ability to promote courage and optimism.

YELLOW

This radiant color of the Sun provides clarity, alertness, and optimism. It helps to align the right use of will.

GREEN

The color of harmony and balance, green corrects imbalance and purifies the nervous system. It is the color of restoration and life. For this reason, time spent among the trees and plants in nature can revitalize and heal.

BLUE

Blue also is restorative and has a calming effect. This color can be used to aid meditation, to enhance inner attunement, and also to relax and restore the nervous system.

PURPLE

This regal color of transformation quickens vibrations, and transmutes what is negative into positive. It strengthens both the nervous and lymphatic systems. Purple also protects the energy vibration of those who wear this color.

The Endocrine System and the Subtle Body

The systems that connect the physical with the subtle in the human body are called the endocrine system and the etheric body, or the "golden web." The etheric body or "the golden web" looks like a beautiful golden web of interconnecting networking which interpenetrates the physical body. This subtle body is nourished by the elements, by beautiful colors, and by thoughts and feelings of both others and yourself. It gives vitality to the physical body and recirculates the life force. If there is disease, it will first manifest in the etheric body as a disrupted energy flow. The point of interpenetration of the subtle and the physical bodies are called in Sanskrit "nadis."

There are seven major energy systems also called "chakras" that exist in the subtle body. Corresponding to these seven energy centers is the endocrine system in the physical body. The endocrine system of the body receives subtle electrical impulses through the vibrations that are emitted, and it sends regulatory messages to the different pathways in the body so that the body can function in a healthy way. The endocrine system also receives messages from the body so that the body can regulate itself if there is a misfunction. There is a saying that "energy follows thought." From the understanding of how the subtle works with the physical, it is possible to see how your thoughts and feelings towards yourself and others will influence your health. It is entirely possible to send healing thoughts to yourself and to have your body respond.

It is also true that gemstones and crystals radiate a vibration due to the energy going through the crystalline structure, as well as the color ray vibration from the stone. This specific vibration goes through the etheric body to the endocrine system and influences the physical body and the emotional body as well.

If you ever need proof of how the body responds to light and color, spend some time in the woods, or by water, or just take time to look at the colors from the sky.

Feed yourself not just the food from the earth, but also the food of the earth, the food of the colors, light, and life of nature, and the spirits of nature.

The Use of Crystals and Gemstones in Past Times

Our heritage spiritually includes the use of crystals and gemstones for varied purposes. It is said the very ancient civilizations of Lemuria and Atlantis used quartz crystals extensively. They were used to generate energy, to heal, to augment mental awareness (crystal headbands were worn on the forehead). It is said that in Atlantis, crystals were used to generate energy, and in fact that the misuse of them helped to cause the destruction of that civilization. But I think it was instead the wrong use of will and a misalignment of purpose that caused the disappearance of Atlantis. It seems that the memories of Atlantis and Lemuria are surfacing now to help us learn the lessons of our own evolution and to come into self-awareness.

Crystals are a bridge for the reawakening of the memories of ancient knowledge. It seems that certain crystals contain coded languages of these ancient civilizations, and perhaps civilizations of intergalactic origins are inscribed in the stones themselves. These coded messages are there for us to read on the intuitive level to accelerate our own understanding. To learn this coded language, as well as the language of nature, is to learn the language of the stones.

Egyptians worked with gemstones in healing. Healing Priests and Priestesses understood the correspondence of certain stones to the chakras, or energy centers, of the body. They understood the refined science of color, light, and sound, and they used these combined methods in their healing work, as did the more ancient cultures. The gemstones most used in Egyptian art were a combination of Lapis Lazuli, Turquoise, and Carnelian. Occasionally Obsidian was used.

Gemstones are specifically mentioned in both the Old and New Testaments. The research of M. T. Ghosn described in his book *Origin of Birthstones and Stone Legends,* determined that the gemstones placed in Aaron's breastplate, according to their patterned design, include: l) Carnelian; 2) Topaz (Citrine); 3) Emerald (Jasper); 4) Ruby (Garnet); 5) Sapphire (Lapis Lazuli); 6) Diamond (Crystal, Beryl); 7)

Zircon (Amber, Turquoise); 8) Agate; 9) Amethyst; 10) Peridot (Green Serpentine, Chalcedony); 11) Onyx (Malachite); and 12) Jasper (Jade). These gemstones helped Aaron in his function as a Priest to transmit energy more effectively and to protect and enhance his own vibrational energy field.

It is quoted in the New Testament that gems were used in the physical foundation of the new city of Jerusalem:

"And I John saw the holy city new Jerusalem coming down from God out of Heaven prepared as a bride adorned for her husband. And the wall of the city had twelve foundations and in the names of the twelve apostles of the Lamb. And the foundations of the wall of the city were garnished with all manner of precious stones. The first foundation was Jasper; the second, Sapphire; the third, a Chalcedony; the fourth, an Emerald; the fifth, Sardonyx; the sixth, Sardius; the seventh, Chrysolite; the eighth, Beryl; the ninth, Topaz; the tenth, a Chrysoprasus; the eleventh, a Jacinth; the twelfth, an Amethyst."

Based on various interpretations, gemstones are said to correspond to the twelve signs of the Zodiac, the twelve tribes of Israel, the Archangels, and the endocrine or chakra system. Corinne Heline, in her book *Healing and Regeneration Through Color,* writes:

"There is a philosophy of color in relation to minerals which has come down to us from anti-

quity, based upon the fact that the twelve zodia-
cal Hierarchies who work with the mineral Kingdom infuse into its component parts something
of the force and rhythm which belong to themselves...The ancients held that every gem was
originally crystallized by and around an enti-
ty...capable of impressing the subconscious
mind of the person possessing the gem as to
coming events, thereby enabling him to avoid
danger and to enhance opportunities. Hence,
the importance of wearing jewels in harmony with
one's stellar rays."

Because the ancient Kabbalists and rabbis
worked in secrecy, conflicting information exists
about birthstones in the Judeo-Christian tradition. However, Mr. Goshn, in his book *Origin
of Birthstones and Stone Legends,* provides a
viable birthstone list:

January	Zircon, Turquoise, Amber
February	Amethyst
March	Jasper, Jade
April	Sapphire, Lapis Lazuli
May	Chalcedony, Agate
June	Emerald, Green Feldspar
July	Sardonyx, Onyx, Malachite
August	Carnelian, Ruby, Garnet
September	Peridot, Light Green Serpentine
October	Beryl, Diamond, Crystal
November	Topaz, Citrine
December	Chrysoprase

The knowledge of gemstones was fully incorporated in the ancient Eastern Indian tradition, whereby practitioners applied their understanding of gemstones to astrological and medical systems; this approach is still utilized in modern times. Because gems are perceived as possessing a special planetary influence, an Indian astrologer looks into an infant's planetary configurations at birth to determine which gemstones will produce beneficial qualities for the child. (Some of the major planetary alignments of gemstones, according to the Indian astrological system, will be further detailed when the properties of gems are discussed in Chapter 3.) The importance given to precious stones also extends beyond astrology in India. In the Indian system of Ayurvedic medicine, gemstones are ground into powder and are prescribed to patients by physicians. This systems of medicine is still practiced today.

The Earth's Magnetic Energy: Gemstone and Crystal Focal Points

The mining location of stones is significant in working with gems, because different areas have unique deposits of trace elements and have varied geological factors. For example, the best Quartz Crystals are found mainly in Arkansas,

Brazil, Madagascar, and Peru. The vibrational qualities of each of these crystals are slightly different. Rubies found in Burma have a deeper, more beautiful color than those mined in Thailand; and Columbian Emeralds are very distinct from those of either Brazil or Africa. Some gemstones, like the Rubies and Sapphires from Sri Lanka, are not mined at all, but are found in the alluvial deposits of river beds.

Because gemstones and Quartz Crystals are focal points for the earth's magnetic field, mining them depletes the earth's vitality. In addition to the removal of gems, the mining of uranium and other metals, as well as oil, is stripping the earth of much of her vibrational quality.

However, positive loving thoughts can help to heal the earth. There is a medical technique that is commonly practiced in England known as "radionics." Practitioners treat a patient by focusing on a sample of the patient's hair or blood and transmitting healing thoughts through the sample. The concept behind this technique is that the same chemical makeup and healing proponents inherent in the blood and hair are similarly expressed in the whole being of the patient. To heal the part is to heal the whole. In this same way, when you wear or work with a gemstone, you are relating to the whole earth; the gem is a focal point of earth's magnetic force that draws to you its energy property.

Conversely, if you send thoughts of Love and

healing to the earth through crystals or gems, these positive vibrations will help to give back to the earth some of what she gives you. This appreciation for and replenishment of the earth is vital if we are to continue living and evolving on her.

Chapter II

Crystals

Crystals are bridges of Light that serve to reflect our own consciousness. They are tools for us to work with. It is important for us to remember that what we are seeking is to become one with our own inner source of Light. Quartz Crystals are one of the most abundant minerals in the earth. As well as the very ancient use of crystals in the lost civilizations of Atlantis and Lemuria, more recent cultures used crystals. If you were to go to Mesa Verde, you could see the tiny Quartz Crystals used by the American Indians to augment their medicine pouches. Crystals were used by the very spiritual tribe, the Chumash Indians, for the purpose of divination. They created a structure with crystals with a fire in the middle, and called this the House of the Sun. The Chinese also used crystals for prophecy. The Tibetans used crystal spheres for very advanced practices in meditation. So we have a vast heritage in the use of crystal by those who preceded us.

One of the crystal's main functions is to increase the ability to intuit, to see, to understand what is not logically understandable. As we are moving vibrationally into a higher manifestation of Light on the planet, we are being called on to develop these hidden and undeveloped faculties. This ability develops the spirit of higher guidance.

Specific Uses of Crystals: Environmental Use

Crystals used in the environment have a special use of augmenting the energy to create a field of strength and protection. The necessity of creating a force field of strength and protection exists because of the toxity in the environment due to pollutants, radiation, international conflicts, and people's fearful and negative thought patterns. The main basis of crystal work is the interfacing that exists between you and the crystal. When you attune to a crystal, you essentially give it the ability to reflect your consciousness back to you.

For this reason before you do any work with crystals, take the time to listen to the crystal, to pray, and to invoke the forces of the Light. When you allow time and space for this inner work to happen, you will get an inner feeling about where to place the crystal in your home or work environment to best serve you. If you have several crystals that you want to place, you are in effect forming a grid pattern around your home or work area. The interrelationship of the formation of the crystals will create a stronger energy pattern. Clusters, groups of crystals, are a very good form to use in your home environment. Also Amethyst, the form of Quartz that is purple, when placed in your home or work space, creates a very strong field of protection. If you do any work with people such as medical, healing, counseling, dental, or organizational work, Amethyst is a very strong form of Quartz to use to keep your environment clean. You can place a prayer in the Amethyst or Clear Quartz that it protect and enhance your work or home place so that your environment becomes a temple of Light for you and others to recharge in.

Because crystals are basic building blocks and focal points of the energy of the earth, the strength and energy will increase the stability of your environment.

Alignment Using Crystals

Through the Law of Correspondence, the luminosity of the crystal is infused with the luminosity of the spiritual Hierarchy. When we focus on crystals, we not only tap into the basic energy patterning which exists in all matter and is imbued with the creative power of all manifestation, we also reflect the Light of our own consciousness back to ourselves. This work helps to align us both physically and metaphysically. When you place crystals in your home environment, you can place your intent into the crystals; in other words, you can pray or place your consciousness in the crystal so that it draws forth what you need to be reflected to you at the time. Because crystals are basic building blocks of Light, you can also ask the crystals to assist you in rebalancing your own life. As the crystals will exist in your environment, this process of self-reflection is a continuous one and will help draw you into a space of more Light and clarity.

Shapes of Crystals

There are many shapes of crystals you can work with. Each shape has its their own special effect. Rough, uncut pieces are good for reading the language of the stones that exists in the crystals in coded messages. Clusters are good for the environment, to purify, to augment, and to lift vibration. Points are good for directional work for focusing energy, and spheres are good for prophecy or having visions. Crystals that have a window formation in them are good for self-reflection, while pyramid shapes are good for drawing energy down from the heavens.

There are special crystals out now for very special purposes, such as the laser wands described in Katrina Raphael's book, *Crystal Healing*. These are like swords of Light and are very powerful tools for this age.

Visioning

Another by-product of inner attunement is the crystal's ability to help us develop inner vision. Crystal spheres are used for this purpose because of the energy of the sphere and the wholeness in its shape. Crystal spheres can also be used to open up your inspiration, or to amplify. To develop the visioning technique is not a matter of "staring into a crystal ball," but rather letting the crystal sphere serve as an object of focus to still the mind and to see beyond the mind and the five senses. Use the sphere as a point of reference; but rather than focus on your vision inside the crystal, focus your vision inside your self and use the crystal as a reference point of your inner self. This is not a process that happens overnight. Rather, it is a gradual attunement. So be patient.

Dreams and Crystals

Dreams are often guide-posts for you, where higher teachings become revealed. However, not all dreams contain guidance. Some act as an outlet to discharge emotion or stress, while others help to heal and to rejuvenate. Learning from your dreams is a skill that needs to be developed. When working with your dreams, keep a notebook by your bed, and write them down as soon as you remember them.

We are at a time in the planet when there is a lot of communication with higher beings through the dream state to instruct us as quickly as we can assimilate it. Crystals can be used to facilitate this process. Place crystals near your bed to create an energy field to draw higher guidance to you from the beings of Light. And once again ask for protection while you sleep so that time can be used most beneficially. Depending on your spiritual orientation, you can call upon the name of Christ, God, Buddha, the Archangels, or any particular saint or teacher whose essence offers you comfort and protection.

Crystals In Your Prayer or Meditation Space

Even if you do not meditate, allow yourself

quiet time alone every day to tune into yourself, to receive whatever guidance is necessary, and, most importantly to still the mind. A special sphere for this purpose is important, because your peaceful energy will accumulate there and will make it easier each time to turn within. Afterwards, you will find that your whole day is charged with this soothing and revitalizing energy. To heighten the energy of this space, your special altar to your higher self or true self, place crystals around or on this special place. Ask them to help hold this energy of Light for you so that you can be in a state of remembrance.

Intuition and Healing With Crystals

Good healers use intuition to follow their higher guidance as they work. Because crystals magnify the energy field, having crystals around and being conscious of their presence will help you to develop your intuition, or a "receptive listening" quality.

Although the force field around the body is affected by the environment, this field is a closed energy circuit. Because crystals transmit energy scientists have, for example, used crystals in watches and radios for a number of years. These stones can help to improve the wiring of the body by strengthening weak circuits and by moving blocked energy.

A healer can place crystals on the body directly or work with crystals on the subtle energy body. Rose Quartz, the crystal that is pink, can be placed on the heart in a healing session to heal the sorrows of the heart. By merely placing the Rose Quartz stone in your environment, you can also enhance the healing vibration of Love, especially when you hold in remembrance the force of Light and Love which activates the crystal's power.

Grid patterns, or patterns of crystals, can be placed around the body to activate the energy flow of the body. You can also heal yourself by holding crystal points that you feel an empathy for against your body on the areas that are blocked or are causing you difficulty. When you place the crystals on your body, visualize your body aligned and being healed with the Light of Divine Love.

Since the mind's function is linked to the endocrine system, other ways to heal yourself include visualizing the cells in your body acting in harmony and visualizing all the cells in your body bathed in Light and healed. Remember that whenever crystals or other gems are used to supplement healing work, it is necessary to cleanse them afterwards with water and to set them in the sunlight.

Healing Circles Using Crystals
More About Grid Patterning

Grid patterning is a very powerful way to work with crystals. The energy that goes from crystal to crystal in the formation of the pattern enhances the crystals. You can place crystals around or in front of you to experiment with the effect of the formation. One way is to place pointed crystals around you in a circle with the points facing in towards you and to put a large generating crystal in the center with you. You can allow your intuition, your inner listening, to tell you where to place the crystals.

Grid patterning with crystals is also very powerful to work with in groups. You can form an energy circle and place the crystals around you on the outside of the circle, all facing inside the circle. You can place a large generator-type crystal or a pyramid in the center of the circle to focus the energy within the circle.

Using crystals to pray for the earth and for peace is a very beneficial aspect of crystal work. A group that forms with this in mind can visualize the planet filled with Light from the forces of Love, from the solar ray vibration. You as a group can send Light and Love to the planet, especially in the areas of stress and assault that she is currently experiencing—that of oil drilling, mining, and radioactive poisoning. Because crystals are such strong vehicles, your prayers for the earth and all beings on the earth will be augmented in strength, and the earth herself will feel the Love that you send to her.

Manifestation Using Crystals

As we move into the New Age, the ability to manifest what is needed on the physical plane through our own power of magnetism will be possible. One of the ways to develop this power is to become aligned with the underlying energy force that exists in all creation. This alignment comes through inner attunement and can be greatly aided by crystals.

Since crystals function as a bridge between the subtle and the physical bodies, by learning to work with crystals you can develop the ability to infuse the stones with your consciousness. Through crystals, your "power of intent"—what it is that you wish to have fulfilled in your life—can be manifested; your consciousness can actually shape the magnetic energy field inherent in crystals according to your thoughts and intention. You are then able to attract "energy" in, for instance, the form of money. However, not only is the ability to manifest money aided when you know what you want to do with the money, but the lesson for all of us in embodiment is to recognize that the power of manifestation is sacred, and its use must be channeled for good purposes that uplift ourselves and others. Many who now serve have realized that this creative process is activated only when there is a balanced flow of energy between giving and receiving.

For the purpose of manifestation, both pointed crystals that direct the flow of energy and crystals with "windows" are powerful tools. Windowed crystals reflect your own feelings of right action and what it is that you want to manifest, whereas pointed crystals increase your ability to act through your own instincts and direct your energy accordingly.

Smoky Quartz

Smoky Quartz plays a unique role in the area of manifestation. Smoky Quartz is the darker colored Quartz of a smoky-colored nature. This particular type of Quartz can be used to attract to you what you need in order to manifest. You can consciously place your intent into the Quartz to bring to you the right people or circumstances to make your manifestation a reality. You can also "program," or place your intention into, the Quartz to form a protective shield so that, whatever you need to manifest, it can be done smoothly and for the welfare of all.

Because of the specific color and trace elements in this form of Quartz, it responds to the intent of radiating to attract to you the right things you need for your aspect of manifestation. This can be done with a group of people together so that you, in effect, set up a telepathic communication to draw to you what you need. This process can also be done with you alone, by setting up one Smoky Quartz near where you sleep and asking it to help you in attracting the right situations and people you need. The power of prayer works to reinforce the reality of the welfare of all involved in your project.

Smoky Quartz, like Amethyst, has the ability to protect your energy field from inappropriate fields of energy. Remember that working with Smoky Quartz will aid you in your manifestation process; and that as we are making the shift of consciousness, manifestation will become increasingly important to us and increasingly available to us.

This aspect of work with crystals is a remembrance of the special technologies that have been used in the past, such as in Lemuria, that are being reawakened now to help in the shift of energy in which this planet is involved.

Wearing Crystals

Just as stones are beneficial for healing

when worn directly on the body, crystals interact with your natural body chemistry to align and balance your energy. Wearing a crystal over the thymus area augments your energy field and attunes your body to the vibration of the crystal. Rose Quartz worn over the thymus gland helps to protect and heal the heart; and wearing this crystal, in particular, produces a calming effect because its vibration is slower than, for example, the Clear Crystal or the Amethyst. The Citrine Quartz is the yellow variety of crystal, and it is good to wear when you have been subjected to chemicals, chemotherapy, or other toxins. The Smoky Quartz, named after its smoky color, in either a rough or cut form activates energy and protects your vibrational field. If you need an extra charge of energy, the Rutilated Quartz is a good crystal to wear; it contains tiny needles that act as rapid conductors of energy.

Many people are attracted to wearing the beautiful Amethyst crystal. The lighter shade of Amethyst is aligned with Jupiter—the planet of spiritual expansion, whereas the darker variety of Amethyst is associated with Pluto—the planet of transformation. In general, the Amethyst's purple color is related to transformation as well. When worn, this crystal can activate the lymphatic system, strengthen the nervous system, and protect the energy field of its wearer. Since the Amethyst is a "soul directional stone," which means that the "soul" purpose of the wearer can be aligned with the crystal, a rough or cut piece placed in the meditation area can also help to accumulate a strong field of meditative energy.

Quartz Crystals can also be used in conjunction with other gems. You can place a gem on a piece of crystal to clean and recharge it, as well as to augment the various properties of the gemstone.

Chapter III

The Healing Properties
of Gemstones

Quartz crystals are a bridge for us to see reflected our own brilliance and the beauty of our inner Light, as well as being a tool for us to focus and direct our energies. Gemstones are more specific and work more in specialized ways for the energy systems in the human body. They are also used as tools to emphasize certain energies; for instance, red stones are good for the heart and the circulatory systems. Gemstones should be worn with an awareness of the effect that they have on you.

Diamond

Diamonds are the most brilliant of all gemstones. They are the hardest (10 on Mohs' scale of hardness). They are formed in the simplest formation of all crystalline systems—the cubic system. Diamonds are carbon that has evolved through millions of years of heat and pressure. They come in many colors: yellow, brown-yellow, green, blue, violet, and pink. When you wear Diamonds, they will both attract energy to you and radiate energy. If you receive a Diamond that had a previous owner, it is a good idea to cleanse the stone with water and Light before wearing it, since Diamonds can keep vibrations in them.

Diamond is in alignment with the Sun. Its brilliance is caused by its ability to refract light. This means simply that Light comes into the stone and is sent out again with even more brilliance. Diamonds are good stones for someone to wear who has personal magnetism, who has the power and energy to initiate projects and resources, who can attract people, and who wants to be in touch with his or her own source of brilliance.

Meditation on the Diamond:
"I am the source of my own brilliance. I am aligned with the inner Sun. I am the source of creativity, of activity, and of right action."

The Corundum Family

The Corundum family is made up of Rubies and Sapphires. Both stones are very powerful.

They have the hardness of 9, the next in hardness from the Diamond.

Ruby

In the Indian astrological system, the Ruby is aligned with the Sun. Because of its red color, it focuses on strength and courage, and it improves circulation. Ruby is found in Burma, Sri Lanka, and Thailand. It is a very powerful stone. Be sure you feel an attraction to wear Ruby, because it is not meant for everyone to wear. For those who are spiritual, the Ruby evokes selfless service, service to the Divine, and pure renunciation. It is the color of Divine Love, of being able to give up what is not necessary for the higher Love.

The word Ruby comes from the Sanskrit word "Ratnaraj," which means "the king of precious stones."

Meditation on the Ruby Red Vibration:
"I am one with the heart of the beloved.
I am able to hear the inner call of selfless
Love and to walk its path."

Sapphire

Sapphire comes in many colors, and its different colors have different energy focuses. The colors we will concentrate on are blue and yellow, but Sapphire comes in pink, greenish-blue, violet, and orange. The rarest and most prized Sapphire is in the orange color, and has the name "Padaparasha," or the lotus-colored Sapphire. Sapphire is found in Sri Lanka, Thailand, and Australia.

Blue Sapphire

Blue Sapphire in the Indian system of astrology is aligned with the planet Saturn. If you have a strong configuration of Saturn in your chart, you might think twice about wearing a lot of Sapphire.

Saturn is the planet of limitation and of testing, but it is also the planet that helps one to learn to give expression in form. In fact the word Sapphire in Sanskrit comes from the meaning, "aligned with the planet Saturn (Sanipriya)." Sapphire, on the positive side, is a stone that King Solomon used for concentration. It is a good stone for writing. Sapphire helps to focus the mind so that it can perceive the truth within the situation, even if the truth is hidden. Sapphire also aligns the wearer with the force of truth and with Love of the truth.

Meditation on the Blue Sapphire:
"I am focused on the higher truth, and all things will unfold in my life according to this focus."

Yellow Sapphire

Yellow Sapphire is aligned with the planet Jupiter, the planet of the spiritual masters, and of expansion in the Indian astrological system. Yellow Sapphire emphasizes the will in relation to the higher Self, or to the highest truth.

Meditation on the Yellow Sapphire:
"I am one with the will of the spiritual master, the spirit of guidance within."

Topaz

Topaz is a wonderful stone. It is aligned with the planet Jupiter, which is the planet of the spiritual masters. Topaz strengthens and aligns the will, recharges the physical body, promotes perception and discrimination as well as optimism and cheerfulness. Topaz is mined in Brazil. Yellow is its most common color. However, more expensive Topaz has an apricot or cherry color. Blue Topaz, which is so popular today, is irradiated in Brazil. Topaz is a beneficial stone for anyone to wear.

Meditation on Topaz:
"I am radiating energy of Love."

Tourmaline

Tourmaline is a very powerful stone that recharges the body. Tourmaline comes from Brazil and California. The colors of Tourmaline are green, pink, watermelon (green and pink together), brown, yellow, and black. Tourmaline is piezoelectric, as is Quartz. The Vikings used Tourmaline to navigate their ships; judges in the Middle Ages held a piece of Tourmaline to help them make their decisions.

Tourmaline should be worn when you feel you need strength or stimulation. Pink Tourmaline brings healing in the form of Love, green tourmaline is restorative, and both colors worn together bring more balance. Tourmaline can also be placed on the body for healing. Tourmaline is the most complex stone, both in the aspect of its crystalline structure and its mineral composition.

The complexity of Tourmaline causes an extra charge to be created in it that necessitates the wearer to be cautious of its power. Because of its complexity, it can draw more complexity. I do not recommend wearing Tourmaline every day. Tourmaline is a powerful stone that has its place in our time.

Meditation on Tourmaline:
"I am able to recharge myself and to direct my focus."

Lapis Lazuli

Lapis Lazuli is found in the inaccessible mountains of Afghanistan, while a lesser quality grade comes from Chile. Lapis was used extensively in Egypt. The Ten Commandments were said to have been engraved in Lapis, and Islamic holy writing was supposed to have been engraved in Lapis as well. Lapis strengthens the skeletal system. Wearing Lapis protects the body and the energy field of the body, and it aids the mind by calming it. It is also a good stone to use for meditation.

Meditation on Lapis Lazuli:
"I am able to calm my mind and strengthen my body."

Garnet

Garnets are very popular stones. They are found in Sri Lanka, Africa, and to a lesser extent, Maine and Idaho. Red Garnets give vitality and increase prosperity and generosity. They vitalize the circulatory system. Orange Garnets offer protection, are energizing, and are also good for the circulatory system. Hessonite, orange-brown Garnet, protect against negative influences, according to Indian astrology. Green Garnets, which come from Africa, are rarer and can be a bit more expensive. They promote optimism as do the other stones in the Garnet family.

Meditation on Garnet:
"I am attracting prosperity."

Peridot

Peridot is a beautiful light green stone, which was greatly respected by the Egyptians. Peridot was called "gem of the sun," and was mined on an island near the Red Sea. Today, Peridot is found in Arizona and Hawaii. It is effective in increasing discrimination.

Meditation on Peridot:

"I am discriminating in my judgment and actions."

Amber

Amber is one of the gemstones that does not consist of crystalline structure. It is a substance from a resin in trees millions of years old. Amber has various colors: light yellow, yellow-brown to brown, and cherry. Amber comes from the Greek word "electron," and in fact, it has an electrical feeling upon the body. It stimulates, heals, and uplifts; it helps to balance glandular functions in the body; and it increases intuition and magnetism. Amber has also been used with dying people.

Meditation on Amber:
"I am radiating healing and Light."

Coral

Coral is made up of tiny skeletal remains of marine life. Gems such as Coral and Pearl that come from the sea help the emotions. Coral helps in the emotion of anger; it alleviates difficult aspects in a person's chart in conjunction with the planet Mars. It is very protective. The most effective color to wear is a dark reddish-orange. Many cultures have valued Coral for its properties. The Chinese, Hindus, Tibetans, American Indians, and the Kahunas have all used Coral for specific purposes in conjunction with their religion.

Meditation on Coral:
"I am in balance with my emotions."

Pearl

Pearl, also from the ocean, helps to purify the emotions. Their very special beauty is caused by an irritation within the oyster. Here is the lesson the Pearls give. Out of irritation and out of friction come translucent beauty and purity. Pearls also refine emotions and can be very absorbing, so it is best not to wear them every day.

Meditation on the Pearl:
"I am here to learn and express the lesson of Love, and refine my emotions so that I understand Love."

Opal

Opal, another gemstone not formed through crystalline structure, is formed by hydrous forms of silica that exhibit a brilliant display of color. It is mined in Australia, where independent miners mine them in very severe climatic conditions. Opal is often indicated if you have a lot of Libra in your astrological chart. Opal can stimulate creativity, inspiration, and intuition. Because it is made up of silica and water, which is not a structured make-up and which is not stable as a crystalline structure, Opal can be difficult for people to wear.

Meditation on Opal:
"I am aware of inspiration and create with it."

Chalcedony

Chalcedony is a family of stones called "Cryptocrystalline Quartz." This means that all members of the Chalcedony family are actually Quartz; but they are opaque, not translucent, and their crystalline structure can only be seen under a powerful microscope. Here are a few examples of Chalcedony:

Agate comes in earth colors, sometimes with

designs on it. There is also a form of Blue Agate that is a very healing stone. Agates are very grounding stones; this means that they keep you regulated with the earth's rhythms.

Bloodstone is a very special stone. It is dark green with small specks of red. The red in bloodstone is supposed to be from the blood of Jesus. Bloodstone, on the physical level, is a blood purifier when worn. Bloodstone is such a healing stone that it will also promote healing on all levels when worn. It also helps in attunement within one's own being. Bloodstone is a beneficial stone for everyone to wear.

Jasper, a dark green stone, is a good general stone to strengthen the body.

Chrysoprase is a light apple green member of the Chalcedony family. It has a beautiful hue to it, and it is healing to the wearer because of its green color. Green is a color that harmonizes.

Green Aventurine is another stone that will assist in general healing due to the green color ray vibration.

Carnelian is a red-orange stone that has very beneficial qualities. It is a strength giver, especially working with the circulatory system. It encourages expression through speech and gives courage. Mohammed, the Prophet, always wore a Carnelian ring. Carnelian is a stone that all can wear.

Sard is a darker version of Carnelian. Its properties are similar.

Meditation on Carnelian:
"I am encouraging to myself and others in my endeavors."

The Beryl Family

It has been said about the Beryl family that the planet Venus seeded these stones, and the Beryl family does indeed emanate a softness. Most Beryl is mined in South America. Its crystalline structure is hexagonal.

Emerald is the most famous, valued, and sought after stone in the Beryl family. It is mined in Columbia, Brazil, and Africa. Emerald was used by the Romans to improve eyesight, and it is also a good stone to wear as a marriage ring. Spiritual initiates used Emerald as a tool for meditation and prophecy.

Meditation on the Emerald ray vibration:
"I am able to see the true aspect hidden within."

Aquamarine is mined in Brazil and Madagascar. It is a soothing stone that can be used for similar purposes as Emeralds. Both stones improve vision physically and on the more intuitive level.

Meditation on Aquamarine:
"I am calm and can emit this gift to others."

Golden Beryl is the yellow member of the Beryl family. It is mined primarily in Brazil, and it is a very beautiful and beneficial stone. Golden Beryl carries the main attributes of stones of the yellow ray vibration: optimism, well-being, and cheerfulness. It also helps attune to the qualities of Love, especially in community affairs.

Morganite is a light pink stone that is also mined in Brazil. It harmonizes and attunes to Love on a universal level.

Goshenite is colorless Beryl. In the Beryl family, the colored gemstones have more effect on the wearer.

The Copper Stones

The next few stones are stones with a high Copper content. I am emphasizing the importance of these stones, because I feel intuitively that Copper protects the body against radioactivity. In the book on gems and their healing properties based on the Edgar Cayce readings, two Copper stones are mentioned quite extensively: Azurite and Chrysocolla. These are the stones that I am most interested in. Here is a listing of a few of the most popular of the stones with a high content of Copper in them. All stones of copper content are opaque, and are soft:

Turquoise

Turquoise, a very popular stone with several cultures, emits a beautiful turquoise color. The American Indians and the Tibetans both used Turquoise and/or the combination of Turquoise and Coral in their jewelry. Turquoise is a porous stone. Because it emits the color of the sky, it encourages a transcendence. The color is also stimulating to the physical body.

Malachite

Malachite is a deep green stone with swirls and bands in it. It is found in Africa and is used both in jewelry and in artifacts. The color in Malachite is very beautiful, and wearing Malachite can be strengthening and stimulating. One thing to note about Malachite is that it is a very absorptive stone, and it can absorb negativity.

Azurite

Azurite is a very healing stone. The color of Azurite is a deep blue. It was mined in Bisbee, Arizona along with copper from the mines; but because the mines in Bisbee have been closed, Azurite is now mined in New Mexico. The deep blue color of Azurite is very beautiful and very healing, and it is a good stone for being able to turn within.

Azurite-Malachite

Azurite-Malachite is a combination stone, and the color of these two stones together is very beautiful. Azurite does not have the same quality of absorption that Malachite does alone, so this combination is a good one to wear and to have in your environment in rough specimens.

Chrysocolla

Chrysocolla is one of the most beautiful and high energy stones there is. The color of Chrysocolla is a beautiful sky blue that stimulates the pineal gland. Chrysocolla is a wonderful stone to have around the house. It is good to keep near you when dreaming, because it is the kind of stone that can connect you to higher realms of consciousness.

Meditation on Turquoise, Azurite or Chrysocolla:
"I listen to the color blue, look at the skies, and sing a song of Love."

Rhodochrosite

Rhodochrosite is a pink stone that comes both opaque with bands, and translucent, which is a bit finer and more expensive. The properties of Rhodochrosite are very healing for anyone who is attracted to wearing it. It heals the heart from past sorrows as do other pink stones, such as Rose Quartz. It also gives a vibration of protection.

Meditation on Rhodochrosite:
"I am able to let go of the past sorrows within my heart, so that I can see all things as new."

Jade

Jade is a stone greatly valued by the Chinese. They say that Jade brings clarity, courage, justice, modesty, and wisdom. Jade is known to be healing for the kidneys. There are actually two kinds of Jade: one is Jadeite, the other is Nephrite. The expensive Jade comes from Jadeite. Nephrite has been used since ancient times; it has in fact been found in ancient burial grounds. Nephrite's color is not as stunning as the good Jadeite. Both varieties of Jade are beneficial to the wearer and can be worn at any time.

Meditation on Jade:
"I am being given the ability to calm my mind, and create right action born out of clarity."

Chrysoberyl

Cat's Eye Chrysoberyl is a very beneficial stone found in the alluvial river beds in Sri Lanka. According to Indian astrology, it counteracts the negative effects of Ketu (the South Node). Cat's Eye Chrysoberyl shows chatoyancy, which is a sharp band of light that runs through the stone. In the best stones, the color of the Cat's Eye is a honey yellow-brown. Cat's Eye protects against dangers, promotes good fortune, and preserves good health.

Meditation on Chrysoberyl Cat's Eye:
"I am protected."

There are other gemstones that exhibit the quality of chatoyancy. Tiger's Eye, a Quartz of similar coloring, has a look similar to that of the Chrysoberyl, but it does not possess the same healing qualities. There is also Cat's Eye Tourmaline, which has similar qualities to Tourmaline, but with more softness.

Stones That Recharge, Aid in Assimilation and Calmness

One way of categorizing stones in terms of balancing the body and psyche is to categorize them as stones that recharge, stones that calm, that absorb, or that aid in assimilation. For instance, if you fatigued easily you would want to wear stones that would recharge you. If you were excited or nervous, you would want to wear a stone that would calm you. If you felt a lot of negativity, you would wear stones to absorb some of that; and if you needed some general assistance in integration, you would wear stones that helped in assimilation.

This is similar to the principles of acupuncture treatment to rebalance energy fields. However, I am writing in generalities, and everyone's state of being is specific; so please once again rely on your own intuition.

Recharging Stones:

Amber, Carnelian, Diamond, Garnet, Ruby, Topaz, and Tourmaline

Stones That Calm:

Azurite, Lapis Lazuli, Pearl, and Rose Quartz.

Stones That Absorb:

Citrine Quartz, Malachite, Pearl, and Rhodochrosite.

Stones That Aid in Assimilation:

Agate, Amethyst, Azurite, Bloodstone, Carnelian, Chrysoberyl, Chrysocolla, Emerald, Jade, Lapis Lazuli, and Quartz

As you can see, it is possible for stones to fall into more than one category. Also, everyone has a slightly different vibrational composition and will react differently.

Quality of Gemstones

Another very important fact to consider is the quality of the crystals or of the gemstone. The clearer the stone is, the more effective it is. In colored gemstones, the better the shade and hue of the color, the better the gemstone.

Wearing Gemstones

Some feel it is good to wear gemstones that are at least two carats for them to have an effect on you. It is good to have the piece of jewelry or the setting of the gemstone with the back open so that you can absorb the vibration of the stone. Where you place the gemstone on your body is significant. On the throat area, or the thyroid gland, it will increase your strength and your self-expression. The thymus gland area, located in the middle of the chest, subtly corresponds to the heart area. This is a very important center for the wearing or placement of gemstones. It is one of the most sensitive areas of the body. Wearing a stone in this area will enhance your energy field.

The next area of great importance is the solar plexus area, which is a significant energy center of the body. It actually does receive energy from the Sun, and it is a nerve plexus center. It is also a center where you subtly receive energy patterns, often in the form of emotions and thoughts from other people. In other words, the solar plexus area both receives and transmits. Both the heart area and the solar plexus area, the two most sensitive areas, or energy centers on the body, were covered by Aaron's Breastplate.

The left side of the body is, in general, the more receptive side, the right side the more active side. If you feel you are very receptive, wearing a silver bracelet on the wrist of the left side would help to protect you; if you feel you need to be more active, wearing a Gold bracelet on the right wrist will give you more direction to work in your endeavors. Both the wrists and the hands contain many small energy centers that correspond to different parts of the body. This correspondence is similar to the correspondence the feet have to the different parts of the body in reflexology.

The Harmony of Gemstones

Gemstones, when worn together, create different energy fields. Aaron's Breastplate exhibited knowledge about the effects of the placement of the different gemstones. This knowledge has been lost. The best thing to do is to be very aware that, when you combine different gemstones, the vibrations and the effects of the individual gemstones will be altered somewhat.

Suggested Gemstones to Wear

Here is a list of gemstones and precious metals to wear on the different energy centers of the body. This is not a definitive list, but rather a suggested list:

Throat-Thyroid Gland
Carnelian: self-expression, courage in speaking.

Lapis Lazuli: inner strength
Diamond: attraction, radiance
Cat's Eye Chrysoberyl: attracts positive
influences

Heart Center Area-Thymus Gland
Diamond: radiance
Yellow Sapphire: alignment with principles of
truth
Lapis Lazuli: strength for body, aid in meditation
Rose Quartz: healing for the heart, both physi-
cally and for sorrows
Rhodochrosite: healing for the heart, and for the
trauma of past sorrow
Jade: calming and healing
Amethyst: protection, recharging, stimulation
Crystal: enhancement of energy field
Azurite: attunement to inner self, protection of
physical body
Chrysocolla: attunement to higher energy, stim-
ulates energy field, protects physical body
Coral: protection against anger
Pearls: purity of emotion
Topaz: strength, radiance, reflection of truth
Aquamarine: calming, soothing

Solar Plexus Area
Golden Beryl: harmony in relations and commu-
nity
Ruby: solar stone, brings in solar energy to re-

charge and strengthen

Topaz: especially good for the heart and solar plexus area

Turquoise and Chrysocolla: good for the heart and solar plexus

The metal for the solar plexus area is Gold. The solar plexus is the energy center of the body that receives energy from the Sun.

Wrist

Metal: can be either Gold or Silver

Tourmaline: recharges, energizes

Fingers

Sapphires

Rubies

Metals in Jewelry

The use of metals for specific purposes is an ancient science that we will touch on briefly. Paracelsus, the great medieval physician, used Gold to strengthen the heart and to purify the blood. He used Silver to treat epilepsy and diseases associated with melancholia. Gold, the most precious (both materially and spiritually) of all of the metals, is aligned with the Sun and the solar forces. The alchemist's dream was to convert baser metals into Gold. Spiritually, this is symbolic of the transformation that we are all a part of, that of transmitting our lower nature into the higher nature. This higher nature is symbolized by the Sun. Gold is the strongest metal to wear; it radiates energy in a way that is similar to the way the Sun radiates energy.

Silver, the metal associated with the moon, can be protective for people who are emotionally sensitive. The moon is associated with the feminine, the emotions, the intuitive.

Synthetic or Treated Gemstones

Some gemstones, such as Ruby and Sapphire, are heat-treated to enhance their color Lapis is often dyed. (The way to check on that is to see if you can see pyrite or calcite markings on the stone.) Some Emeralds are oiled to enhance their color, while Blue Topaz is irradiated. Usually it is a colorless Topaz before they irradiate it.

I do not recommend irradiated stones as they still might emit radiation. Other stones that are irradiated are Quartz Crystal. They take on a brownish-yellow color when they receive this treatment.

Rubies and Sapphires can be made synthetically. It is hard to tell synthetic Rubies from natural rubies. A good gemologist can tell by taking the stones through a number of tests. Basically, just be aware that there are various ways in which stones can be adulterated.

Chapter IV

Windows of the Past, Windows of the Future

Power Spots on the Earth

The earth has certain energy centers on it, just as the human body has energy centers. These centers are related and correspond to one another. Ancient ones understood this correspondence and built structures on some of these energy centers. These structures include Stonehenge and other stone circles in England, the Pyramids, Macchu Picchu, and the mysterious landing lines that exist in the Andes. Ley lines in England have been found by dowsers to connect with underground lines of magnetism that connect stone circles together throughout the country.

These structures were built to be in alignment with planetary movements, and in some instances (such as the landing fields and lines in the

Andes), they looked like they were forms of communication with intergalactic beings. The sacred science of numbers and measurements was built into the structures, as evidenced in the Pyramids. There is a legend, in fact, that the top of the Pyramid had Gold and a great crystal to draw in energy from the heavens to the earth.

As we enter the New Age, these ancient power centers will be paid increased homage, and thus, activated. This interest and prayer will help to align the earth's energy field during the coming shift so that the earth will stabilize. People who pray for peace at these spots and who wish to join with others in the same prayer will help to create lines or grid patterns of Light throughout the planet.

There are other important power centers on the earth that do not have structures on them. These centers include Mt. Shasta; the Haleakala crater in Maui; the sacred mountain of Taos, New Mexico; the Himalayas; and many others. The energy of the sacred in relationship to these places on the earth will gain more and more interest as we spontaneously remember the ways of our ancestors, who built structures that we are just on the verge of understanding.

How To Find Your Own
Power Spot

The Indian systems described small energy centers called "nadis" as well as major energy centers called "chakras." The earth has these centers as well and can activate, revitalize, heal, and align beings who live on her and partake of her. These sacred power places exist all over the planet. All you have to do to find your place is to listen to your intuition, to your own heart for guidance.

Several years ago, I was living in the country in Amherst, Massachusetts. One night I took a ride alone in my car and found myself driving to an area where I had never been before. I found myself by a stream that was very beautiful and healing. I intuitively knew that the stream was a sacred spot; that I was made aware of it so that I could have a place to regenerate myself. For the remainder of the time that I was in Amherst, I could go to the stream and refresh myself and be healed. Wherever you live now, unless it is right in the middle of the city, there is a special spot for you that the earth provides. To give back to the earth and to the nature spirits that live there, bring an offering of Love such as fragrant fruit, or leave a small crystal there and say a prayer for the earth and her abundance.

Recently I took a trip to Maui. I went up to

the Haleakala crater and definitely felt the presence of the rainbow Gods who live there. I learned of the legends of the Hawaiian rainbow Gods and knew that this was true, that there were, in fact, rainbow Gods. I felt totally restored when I returned home, and I still feel in touch with that spot.

Reconnection to your power spots, both major and minor, will reconnect you to yourself.

Working With Crystals in Nature

You can create grid patterns in nature to help you focus yourself. When you do this, you can use the solar energy to help create these grid patterns. Bridges can be formed, as well as interconnectedness to the crystals, with the use of the Sun and the shadows that are cast.

Abundance

We live in a time of fear of scarcity, generated by the consciousness of lack and of fear. Yet, the earth in her abundance gives everything that we need to survive and to grow in knowledge. There is enough food right now for everyone on the planet to eat, and there are enough resources for everyone to be taken care of. The main problem is the idea of scarcity and greed in man's own consciousness. To remember the earth and everything that she provides is one step towards abundance. Abundance is first a state of awareness. It is understanding that abundance is not only about money or about survival, it is everything in your life.

Self-Acceptance

It is very hard to conceive of receiving abundance in your life if you do not feel that you are worthy of receiving abundance, or of manifesting abundance. The work we are collectively involved with is self-acceptance. Self-acceptance means feeling worthy to receive the good that the universe has to offer us, and it also means to accept others with Love. This does not mean do not be discriminating; because of the shift on this planet, it is more important than ever to be discriminating. Self-acceptance means to honor who we really are, what is underneath the facade of the personality, what we are in fact created from which is pure Light and truth. Crystals help us achieve self-acceptance by reflecting our own brilliance, for it is our own brilliance that we long to acknowledge.

If we do not cultivate self-acceptance, we will not be able to see clearly what opportunities we should participate in and what opportunities we should avoid. We will misjudge people; we will not be able to create abundance or to manifest what we need to manifest. Even if we do all the right things on the outside, if we do not have inner Love for ourselves in our own hearts and do not have Love for others, we will not be able to flow with the energy. We have to think about what we project to the world, since the world is a mirror to us. No amount of money will change our feelings of personal failure. As we learn self-acceptance through the lessons on our earth's journey, we can open to receive the abundance the earth herself is made of. As we radiate Love, we can also attract Love.

The Crystal Healing Temple: A Visualization Exercise

Take time to allow your body to be comfortable and to relax. Let your daily concerns, your worries, float away. For this time, allow yourself to feel totally supported by the Love of which the universe is made manifest.

You can now take the time and the space to remind yourself that there is no lack in the universe, that you are worthy. Allow yourself to feel sustained by Light and by Love. Forgive your-self for any errors you may have committed and know that they were done in ignorance, and for-give others any hurts that they did to you know-ing that they also acted out of ignorance or fear. Allow yourself the opportunity to see that every-thing you see is a manifestation of the same Light and the same Love that you are made up of.

In this sacred space where everything is suf-ficient, begin to visualize a crystal temple of healing. Begin to visualize the temple made up of crystals, crystals huge and small, from this plan-et and from other planets. Feel the vibration of the crystals and see the brilliance of the Light as they are reflected through the crystals. Allow yourself to walk into this crystal healing temple. As you walk into this temple, begin to hear the beautiful tones and see the beautiful rainbow colors that crystals emit. The sound and the color are for your healing, for the cells in your body to align themselves in a healthy way, and for your consciousness to understand the prin-ciples of manifestation. For the sound and the light emanating through the crystal stimulate your own sense of completeness.

Allow yourself time to look around the temple and see what this temple made up of crystal and Light looks like. As you align yourself with the energy of the crystal, remind yourself that there is no scarcity. Let yourself see that you are an expression of perfection, and that your life is an outer expression of the Love that is you. Let yourself feel your heart, and let your heart reflect Light like the crystal. Understand that there is no lack, there is only completeness manifesting in form, and completeness that manifests through you. Let your heart reflect the light of the crystal. And from within the heart, sing the song that needs to be sung.

Healing Meditation: The Crystal Rose

Place your consciousness in your heart, fill your heart with Light, and let yourself remember hurt that you have felt in the past from other people. Allow your consciousness to take you back to the healing temple where you are surrounded by the crystals. Let yourself feel the hurt, and then turn your attention to a rose, a beautiful perfect rose that is unfolding. Visualize the rose in the heart as an expression of unfolding Love, as Love expressing itself through the patterns in your life. Let the beauty of the rose help you forgive those who have hurt you in your past. As you forgive others, so also forgive yourself for mistakes you have made. Let the feeling of forgiveness move in your heart.

As you forgive yourself and others from past

hurts, you will allow more Love to express yourself through your heart, and you will experience abundance in your life. Once again visualize the crystal rose, the rose of perfect Light, and Love yourself as you are, and allow yourself to Love others as they are. Just as a crystal or gemstone has its inclusions and imperfections that occurred during its formation, you also are in a learning process. Once again, allow yourself the space to forgive yourself and others and visualize yourself as becoming one with the crystal rose. Let this expression of Love reflect itself through you to others through the heart.

Windows of the Past; Windows of the Future

We are at the point in time when we are about to make a shift in consciousness on this planet. The crystals that we are so attracted to are reminders of our inner brilliance, which we will see reflected out, as well as reminders of our heritage. The crystals are our windows to our self and they are windows of our past and windows of our future.

The heritage of our past, of the civilizations that remain only in legend and in memories, is being reawakened as we prepare for our next necessary step in evolution. It is true that what we see reflected we can work with. The crystals serve as contact points of our higher selves, of our inner Light, so that we can be aware and keep serving and reawakening. The memories of the past, of great civilizations where giants walked, where beings were telepathic and highly evolved, where thoughts were immediately made manifest, where healing was done in a holy way using crystals, gems, Light, and sound—this is our heritage, this is where many of us come.

Why have these civilizations come and gone? What collective memories and guilt do we feel in the passing of civilizations? The answer to these questions can only be known by looking within. Every step in our process of coming home, of coming to know the self, is a necessary one. We will remember the knowledge that we once had access to, we will remember and work with the mysteries of the past. But we will remember in a new way. We are going to remember the heritage of our ancient days so that we can reawaken and move into the future without fear, and with anticipation of manifestation of Light and Love that we all long for deep within our hearts.

The ancient ones who came before us, those who built structures that currently defy our capability, who honored the ways of the mystery schools where the workings of spirit and matter were combined in service and homage, these ancient ones are our ancestors, and this knowledge is our inheritance. Ours is an inheritance of plenty; it is an inheritance of the sacred married to the mundane; it is an inheritance of the many made manifest through the one; it is an inheritance teaching us to believe what we are, in fact, capable of. This knowledge, this remembrance is in the stones, programmed by advanced beings, and it is also within our hearts. The windows of the future will be opened because we are at the point of the next step. It is knowledge that is written within ourselves that will assist us in the next step our evolution holds for us. The ancient mysteries are within us, and we will learn from them and come to a new level of awareness. We will relearn how to align ourselves with the solar, planetary, and intergalactic energy. We will relate to the earth in a sacred way and learn that abundance comes in all forms and there is no limit to the endless streams of Light and Love that can be made manifest.

We will become aware of our great capabilities in telepathy, in empathy, and in learning how to recharge ourselves, so that we can move into the future without fear, but instead, with remembrance of what we have been, of our great feats and accomplishments.

The knowledge of the past is re-emerging so that the way of the future will be made known. We will learn that our birthright is not the way of destruction but the way of emergence in the Light so that we can create, and ourselves become bridges so that the new ways will emerge.

We will sit in circles with the Sun and use our tools of Light to align the forces on this planet. The time of true fulfillment will manifest, and we will greet one another as the true vessels of Light that we are.

Quotations in book reprinted with permission:

M. T. Ghosn
Published by Inglewood Lapidary
P.O. Box 70l
Lomita, California 90717

Corinne Heline
DeVorss & Co.
P.O. Box 550
Marina del Rey, California 90294

Pat Dongvillo

Miriam Kaplan is available for workshops on crystals. For scheduling information please write:

Julia Saiber Heyman
P.O. Box 954
South Orleans, MA 02662

Index